WRITE THIS WAY

WRITING
POWERFUL
PERSUASIVE
PIECES

NANCY LOEWEN

LERNER PUBLICATIONS ◆ MINNEAPOLIS

Lerner Publications Company
A division of Lerner Publishing Group, Inc.
241 First Avenue North
Minneapolis, MN 55401 USA

For reading levels and more information, look up this title at www.lernerbooks.com.

Main body text set in Dante MT Std 12 / 15. Typeface provided by Monotype.

Library of Congress Cataloging-in-Publication Data

Loewen, Nancy, 1964-
    Writing powerful persuasive pieces / by Nancy Loewen.
        pages cm. — (Write this way)
    Audience: Ages: 11–14.
    Audience: Grade 7–8.
    ISBN 978-1-4677-7906-7 (lb : alk. paper) — ISBN 978-1-4677-8288-3 (pb : alk. paper) — ISBN 978-1-4677-8289-0 (eb pdf)
    1. Persuasion (Rhetoric)—Study and teaching (Middle school)—Juvenile literature. 2. Composition (Language arts)—Juvenile literature. 3. English language—Composition and exercises—Juvenile literature. 4. Language arts (Middle school) I. Title.
    P301.5.P47L69 2016
    372.62'3—dc23   2014046773

Manufactured in the United States of America
1 – VP – 7/15/15

Table of Contents

INTRODUCTION

You have hidden powers.

You can change what people think. You can change what people do. You might even be able to change what people believe—about themselves, their lives, and even the world itself.

Skeptical? Think about all the times you've talked your parents into ordering pizza. Maybe you convinced them to let you have a dog or to increase your allowance. Maybe you sold a crazy amount of coupon books to raise money for your school. Maybe you helped two quarreling friends talk things through.

You have powers of persuasion.

In this book, you'll learn how to take all of that power and amplify it—through writing. When you know how to write persuasively, your influence extends beyond your own family and friends. You can reach people you don't know well. You can reach people you've never even met!

Persuasive writing has changed the course of history. Here are just a few examples:

1776—Thomas Paine published the pamphlet "Common Sense," which urged the American colonies to assert their independence from Great Britain. We all know how that one turned out.

1962—*Silent Spring*, by Rachel Carson, convinced people that pesticides—particularly DDT—were harmful not just to insects but to birds, fish, and people as well. The book

marked the start of the modern environmental movement.
1965—Ralph Nader's book *Unsafe at Any Speed* prompted
the federal government to set standards for auto safety.
In the years following the book's release, the government
began requiring car manufacturers to install seat belts, air
bags, and other safety features in their vehicles.
1987—Randy Shilts published *And the Band Played
On*, which argued that apathy and incompetence
among government officials allowed AIDS to become
an epidemic. The book led to more research and
government policies that helped contain the disease.

OK, maybe you're not *quite* ready to change the world with
your writing. But persuasive writing still has a place in your
life—and not just in school. Have you ever gotten mad about
a company's policies? You could write a letter to the company
president and complain. Maybe you're trying to start a petition in
your community and you need to write a convincing description
of your cause. Even tweets and Facebook posts can influence the
thoughts and behavior of others.

The Greek philosopher Aristotle identified three main
aspects of persuasion: *logos* (logic), *ethos* (credibility), and *pathos*
(emotion). Basically, if you want to persuade people, you need to
appeal to their minds and their hearts—and you need to assure
them that you are worth listening to.

This book will give you the tools you need to write a
convincing persuasive piece. Some of the advice is about how to
conduct research. Some of it is about the writing process. That
information will help you with all kinds of nonfiction writing—
or any kind of writing, actually. But this book also describes
the many methods of persuasion you can use to convince other
people to start thinking your way.

Persuasive writing puts you in charge. You have the power.
Use it wisely!

WHAT'S YOUR TOPIC?

Whether you're writing a blog post, a five-paragraph essay, or a twenty-page research paper, here's the most important step in writing a great persuasive piece: pick a topic you care about. Don't pick a topic because you think it will be easy—you'll get bored and end up with a boring piece. Writing isn't always easy and it isn't always fun, but it can be incredibly satisfying. And the more passionate you are about your topic, the better your piece will be. Why? Because it's a reflection of that passion.

FIRE UP!

Maybe you're already revved up about a cause or topic and you can't wait to get going. That's great. But if nothing comes to mind right away, no worries. There are lots of ways to generate ideas. Consider one of these suggestions:

- Tune in to current events. Read the newspaper for a few days. Watch the news on TV or browse respected news sites on the Internet. Which stories hold your attention?
- Make a list of things that make you mad—really mad! Whether you focus on school or friendships or

family life or activities or politics, it doesn't matter. You can often connect the things that make you mad in your personal life to a larger theme.

- Make a list of things that make you feel great. Could you connect these things to a larger theme as well? Try filling in the blank: *The world would be a better place if* _____.
- Consider the rules in your family, school, and community. Think about state and federal laws too. How have those rules or laws affected you or someone you know? Is there a rule or law that your community (or country) needs?
- What about arguments at the family dinner table? When you have get-togethers with your extended family, do any topics make sparks fly?
- Think about the athletes, actors, authors, and other people you admire. Do any of them speak out about causes that matter to you?
- Look at a tiny part of your life under a microscope and brainstorm questions. Take breakfast, for example. Do you have a strong opinion about organic or locally grown food?

Write down all of your ideas. Don't stop to evaluate them. You'll have time for that later. You might find connections between your topics that lead to even more ideas.

When you're done gathering your ideas, take a close look at your notes. Which topics would you like to learn more about? Which ideas are unique? Which are most relevant to your life? Soon you'll need to get very specific about your topic. But for now, it's OK to be general. This is the starting point.

GET AN OVERVIEW

When you're covering a complicated topic, it's a good idea to get a broad overview at the start of your writing process. Do you or your parents ever look up directions on the Internet? You can zoom in or zoom out for different levels of detail. Developing an overview is like zooming out on a map. You're looking at the major roads and trying to figure out where your destination is in relation to other states, cities, neighborhoods, or landmarks.

The Internet will likely be your first stop as you begin your research as well. That's OK, but at this point, don't dig in too deeply. Just skim—otherwise, you might be so overwhelmed with information that your search is more confusing than helpful. You're just trying to get a sense of how much information is out there.

An encyclopedia might be a better place to begin. Encyclopedia entries are generally short and reliable. Look at more than one encyclopedia, if possible. They might include slightly different information. (You can always try Wikipedia too, but don't depend on that one resource.) And keep in mind that the words you're using might not match exactly with the headings in the encyclopedia. Try different words until you find what you need. If your topic is very current or very specific, however, you might not find anything in an encyclopedia.

Nonfiction books for younger readers can be another great way to get an overview. You can browse them quickly and get a feel for how the information is organized. They often mention websites and other books that you can turn to for more information. And they have lots of cool pictures!

Should you be taking notes at this point? That's up to you. If taking notes helps you remember the major roads and landmarks, go for it. If you feel you know the territory, notes aren't essential—yet. Whatever approach you take, be sure to write down any sources that you may want to come back to. That way, you'll know where to find them later.

Now that you've looked at the big picture, are you still feeling excited about your topic? Are you overwhelmed by the information available? Or are you concerned you won't find enough? It's not too late to change your mind. Getting an overview is a way to find out if your topic is a good fit for you.

ARGUMENT AND AUDIENCE

As you move forward with your piece, there are two questions you should be asking yourself: What is your thesis, or argument? And who is your audience? The answers will provide direction for both your research and your writing process.

Your thesis statement informs the reader of your main point and how you intend to make your case. It should be carefully worded and specific. You probably aren't ready to write your thesis statement yet, but a sense of purpose will serve you well.

After all, in a persuasive piece, you're not merely providing information or saying what's on your mind. You want your readers to change their beliefs or take action. The outcome is either success or failure.

Your purpose is connected to the audience you're writing for. Who are you trying to reach? If you're writing a letter to the editor for your local paper, you're addressing people of all ages who live in your community. If you're writing for your school paper, you're addressing your classmates and teachers. Or maybe you want to write a guest blog post on an organization's website for a specialized group such as dog owners or hockey families. Take time to think about who will be reading your piece. What do these people have in common? What knowledge do they have? What experiences do they share?

As you continue to research, remind yourself of your audience. Picture yourself onstage, with your readers sitting in front of you, waiting to hear what you've got to say. What would make them yawn or fidget? What would get them to nod or crack a smile?

WRITE IT OUT!

Once you have a general idea of your topic, brainstorm all the questions you can think of. Challenge yourself by looking at the topic from a point of view other than your own. What questions would you ask if you were elderly? Or a person of a different race or ethnic background? If you lived in a rural area or in a big city? If you practiced a different religion? If you had a disability? Don't judge your questions—just jot them all down. This exercise might open your mind to possibilities you hadn't considered.

LEARN FROM THE MASTERS

In this passage from a blog post by Hmong American writer Kao Kalia Yang (below), Yang gives her readers a look into

why a topic matters to her. Before discussing a hurtful depiction of Asian Americans on TV, Yang demonstrates how the program prompted thoughts about her past—and her daughter's future:

Last night, I turned on the television to watch the Golden Globes . . . When I was younger, my older sister Dawb and I used to watch the Golden Globes together. We didn't get to go to the movies because our parents couldn't afford it but we wanted to know how to talk about certain films with our friends at school. It felt like a magical world far away from the government subsidized houses we and our extended Hmong family knew as America. . . . Dawb and I watched side by side, weeping at the moments when the winners thanked their families, reflected on their long journeys, and graced the world with their bits of wisdom. I thought it would be fun to watch the Golden Globes last night, my little girl at my side, share some of what life could look like if one's dreams came true.

Of course, at this point, you might not know the form you'll use or the audience you're trying to reach. That's not a problem— you're just starting out. Some writers may need to write a very general draft or two before they make these choices. Just be aware that eventually you'll need to make a decision about your mission and your audience in order to write a piece that's truly convincing.

FIND YOUR SOURCES

Once you've gotten an overview and committed to your topic, the next step is to gather your research materials: books, magazines, newspapers, blog posts, documentaries, news clips, and so on. You don't need to read every word, though. At this point, you're just trying to determine if a particular source will be useful for you. Can you understand it without having to look up words in the dictionary every few sentences? Does it make you want to learn more?

You'll probably look up sources on the Internet to start with. To save time, be specific with your search terms, using specialized words associated with your topic whenever possible. Another good way to begin: talk to a reference librarian. Explain what you need, and chances are, the librarian will know just where to look. You can also access articles through a library website instead of relying on Google or another search engine. That way, you'll cut down on the irrelevant stuff.

No matter where you track down your sources, be sure they are credible—that is, capable of being believed. If you want to get the facts about the latest "miracle food," which would be a better choice: a gossipy tabloid or the science section of the *New York Times*? Determining the credibility of a source can be a challenge. Sometimes respected sources don't look all that different from questionable ones. If you're not sure a source is reliable, ask a parent, a teacher, or a librarian. You could also

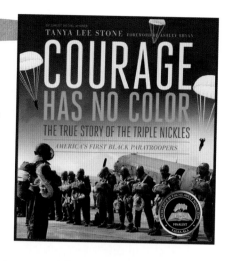

consult a website called *NewsTrust* (newstrust.net), a nonprofit site that rates news sources for trustworthiness.

Pay close attention to the authors of the books or articles you're considering. Avoid articles that don't list an author, unless they come from well-established organizations such as universities or government agencies. If you're covering a serious topic, the authors you select should be respected in their fields, with credentials that may include advanced degrees and publication credits. Don't rely on self-published books, unless it's very clear that the author's credentials are solid. Self-published books may appear to have a publisher, so do a quick search of the publisher's name as well. A traditional publisher will have many books in print, not just a few.

Sometimes the same information appears in multiple places on the Internet. Try to track down the original source. If you find a compelling statistic on a blog, look for a hyperlink—it may take you to the person or organization that created the content. (If there isn't a hyperlink or a citation, think twice about using the statistic.) Another important tip: note the copyright or publication date of your sources and use the most current information available. **Basing your argument on outdated information will make your piece irrelevant, no matter how well it's written.**

If you don't find a lot of information about your topic, see if there's an industry magazine or organization that is connected to your topic. The US government publishes a list of consumer and trade organizations (http://www.usa.gov/topics/consumer /trade-organizations.pdf) that could put you on the right track. You may need to contact an organization directly to get the information you need. Good sources often lead to additional good sources, so follow the information trail!

Even if you're writing a short piece, keep track of your sources. That way, if you realize that the perfect quote was in an article you looked at three days ago, you'll at least have a place to start looking. Record details such as the title, author, publisher, date of publication, and web address. Having this information at your fingertips will make citing your sources easier later on.

PRIMARY AND SECONDARY SOURCES

Sources are divided into two main categories: primary and secondary. Books, articles, and documentaries by people who weren't present for or directly involved with a topic are examples of secondary sources. If you want to take your piece to a higher level, consider using one or more primary sources.

A primary source is original material created at the time and place you're writing about. These sources give an inside view of a topic. Diaries, speeches, manuscripts, letters, legal documents, and interviews are examples of primary sources.

Firsthand interviews, in particular, can be a terrific addition to a piece. You'd be generating content no one has ever seen before! Maybe you're lucky enough to know someone who's a good subject for an interview. Your uncle is a chemical engineer, for example, or your neighbor works for a company that manufactures solar panels. But you don't have to be on a first-name basis with

LEARN FROM THE MASTERS

Many rare primary documents have been scanned or recorded and are available online for anyone to see. For example, on the National Archives government website, you can view a letter that baseball player Jackie Robinson (below) wrote to President Dwight D. Eisenhower in 1958. Robinson urged Eisenhower to take a strong stand on civil rights. Check out the opening lines of Robinson's letter and then find the rest online: "My dear Mr. President: I was sitting in the audience at the Summit Meeting of Negro Leaders yesterday when you said we must have patience. On hearing you say this, I felt like standing up and saying, 'Oh no! Not again.'"

someone to get an interview. Many people—even high-ranking experts—are willing to help students out. In-person interviews are an excellent opportunity, if you can arrange one, but you can also conduct your interview via phone, e-mail, or video chat. In the research you've already done, maybe you've come across organizations, authors, or university programs connected to your topic. Don't hesitate to send an e-mail and ask for assistance.

WRITE IT OUT!

Surveys (on paper or online) allow you to create one-of-a-kind content for your piece and deepen your understanding of your topic. In fact, writing the questions for a survey— whether or not you actually conduct it—is a great exercise to get you thinking about your topic. If you're writing about the need for a community garden, for example, you could start out with questions like these:

- Do you think our town would benefit from having a community garden?

- Would you personally rent a plot?

- What is the most you would spend?

- How often would you be able to go to the garden?

- How far would you be willing to drive to get to the garden?

Think about the variety of people who would be answering your questions. Anticipate what their concerns might be.

If you do get an interview, be prepared. Don't waste time—yours or your expert's—by asking general questions that you should already know the answers to. The more familiar you are with your topic, the more insightful your questions will be. And word your questions in a way that invites an in-depth answer, as opposed to yes or no. "What are the challenges of your job?" would be a better question than "Do you like your job?"

Maybe you'd like input from people who aren't experts. You're trying to understand how an event or situation affects ordinary people. You could set up a focus group and interview many people at once. Or you could conduct a poll, survey, or experiment. Maybe a visit to a museum—or a zoo or the mall—is in order! Research isn't just looking things up in books and articles. Research means exploring your topic in a way that makes it come alive.

READ TO LEARN

You've rounded up most of your sources. You have a decent idea of what will work as evidence for your position. Here comes the fun part.

Read.

Just read.

This is a subject you care about, so learn all you can. If possible, read through your material two or three times! You'll wait a bit to begin writing, but once you start, the rest of the process will go smoothly. You'll remember the material well and have plenty of confidence as you go to the next step.

CHAPTER 3

COLLECTING EVIDENCE

By now you know plenty about your topic, but you might be wondering how you'll ever end up with a polished, well-organized piece. How can you begin to corral your thoughts into some kind of logical structure? Begin with a brainstorm. Simply write down everything you can think of about your topic. You might not remember the exact facts and figures, but that's OK—you would need to confirm those later anyway. Just put it all out there, in no particular order. Be sure to include the questions you still have about your topic too. When you honestly can't think of one more thing, examine your list. Could you group any ideas together?

MAKING CONNECTIONS

Let's say you're writing in favor of a shorter school day. Here are some of your thoughts:

- Would give kids more time to do homework
- Kids could help out more at home
- Teachers would have more time to prep for the next day
- Older kids with jobs could work more if they need to
- Kids would get more sleep because they could finish their homework earlier in the day

- Con: families with young kids would need more day care
- Kids would feel less pressure
- What do other countries do?
- More flexibility with school start times/busing schedules
- Story about an overscheduled kid

If you look closely, you may start seeing some connections. How many of these ideas relate to emotional health? How many relate to student performance? How many relate to teachers or finances? Arrange your notes into whatever categories you decide to use. Later, you might add new ideas and eliminate others. You might even add or eliminate entire categories. But you're off to a good start!

CLEAR AND SPECIFIC

Ideally, you still have a vision of how your passion for your topic will affect your readers. However, while you might be thinking *I want all of you to drop everything and do what I say, because this is important!*, you can't put it like that in your piece. So as you sort your ideas, think about your central argument. **A solid thesis statement is clear and specific. If your argument is too broad, readers won't find it compelling.** An unfocused thesis can actually make your research more complicated, because you will have many paths to follow. If you were a detective trying to solve a crime, would you rather have a few likely suspects or dozens of them?

In addition to being clear and specific, a thesis statement should be debatable—that is, it should indicate that there are other sides to the issue. You aren't simply stating a fact or describing what your piece is about. You are informing readers of the boundaries of your argument.

LEARN FROM THE MASTERS

In this excerpt from *Our Choice: A Plan to Solve the Climate Crisis*, author (and former vice president) Al Gore addresses a potential objection to wind turbines: that birds will be killed. Note how he puts the issue into perspective while still acknowledging that wildlife is important.

Al Gore (above) published *Our Choice: A Plan to Solve the Climate Crisis* in 2009.

Some people worry about birds being killed when they fly into the blades of wind turbines. No one likes to see wildlife killed, but let's look at the facts. Thousands more birds are killed each year by flying into skyscrapers, by house cats, and by automobiles and pesticides than by windmills. On the other hand, stopping the climate crisis by cutting fossil fuel use will save whole species of birds from extinction. Still, engineers are working on ways to cut down on bird deaths from windmills. One solution is a sensor that will shut down the turbine when it detects a flock of birds.

Let's look at the shorter school day example. "Many countries have shorter school days than we do in the United States" wouldn't be an effective thesis because it's not debatable. It doesn't take a position. "Shorter school days would be good for students" isn't strong either, because it's not specific. But if you wrote, "Our school district should adopt a shorter school day in order to improve student and teacher performance and to provide a better quality of life for families," you would be on the right track. Your position is clear, and you are letting the reader know the main points of your piece. It's also debatable—someone could argue that a shorter school day *wouldn't* lead to those benefits.

SUPPORTING EVIDENCE

No matter how eloquently you express yourself, your persuasive piece will fall flat if you don't support your ideas with evidence. Think about your own life. Don't you hate it when adults tell you "just because" or "because I said so" instead of giving you a real explanation for what you're being asked to do? You might not always agree with their explanation, but at least you know where they're coming from.

In a persuasive piece, the basic types of evidence you're likely to use are facts, statistics, and expert testimony. A fact is a credible piece of information—something that people know or can verify. Some facts are straightforward. (Kansas became a state in 1861. Lake Erie is the southernmost lake of the five Great Lakes. Earth revolves around the sun.) But it's not always easy to tell fact from fiction. Sometimes we believe statements are facts when they really aren't. For example, many people think that Betsy Ross made the first American flag. But we don't know that for sure! A relative credited Ross with making

This detail from a nineteenth-century painting depicts Betsy Ross sewing the American flag. However, we lack historical evidence that proves this happened. The story of Betsy Ross is an example of people mistaking speculation for fact.

the flag nearly a century after the flag made its debut, but there's no historical proof. So pick the most credible, up-to-date sources you can find. Scientists, historians, and researchers of all kinds are constantly adding to our body of knowledge.

Statistics express information as numbers or percentages. They're another way to bolster your argument. People use statistics to summarize data from all areas of life, from classroom science experiments to the US population census. As with facts, choose current, credible sources of statistics. Don't cite a scientific study from a blog filled with typos and pop-up ads. A better choice would be a government agency or a scientific institution. Also, keep in mind that even the most reliable, startling statistics might not make your case completely. People can—and often do—draw different conclusions from the same set of numbers.

Your persuasive piece should convey your own individual voice, but that doesn't mean you can't use expert testimony. Get some help from someone who is an authority in a field of study that's relevant to your topic. A compelling quote may convince your readers that you're on the right track. Using quotes here and there is also a good way to add variety to your piece and keep your readers engaged.

Personal stories and quotes allow your reader to make an emotional connection to your topic. In *Immigration: The Ultimate Teen Guide*, Tatyana Kleyn *(right)* includes quotes from immigrant teens. This quote by sixteen-year-old Alisher, who is from Uzbekistan, appears in a chapter called "Encountering Discrimination." Alisher's words give readers a better understanding of some of the issues that immigrant teens face.

> When I first arrived there were many students who were making fun of my accent. When I say I am from Uzbekistan they are very ignorant because they didn't know the country so they are mixing it up with Pakistan and things like that. They also say that I am from Japan. That makes me feel upset because I didn't know that I would be treated this way when I came here.

WIRED FOR STORIES

Facts, statistics, and expert testimony will earn you the respect of your readers. But to fully persuade readers, you should appeal to their emotions as well. Stories are a great way to do that. You could relate your own experience or someone else's. People may forget facts and figures, but if they relate to a story, they will be more likely to agree with your position. Our brains are wired for stories—think of cave drawings and ancient myths. Even in the twenty-first century, a time of countless ways to communicate, a story is still one of the best ways to share information and elicit an emotional response.

Let's say you're writing about the need to be prepared for a natural disaster. You describe the hardships a particular family faced when their electricity was off for five days following a hurricane. You include some direct quotes from family members. With those moves, you totally amp up the persuasive power of your piece.

WRITE IT OUT!

In writing a persuasive piece, you are constructing an argument. Effective persuasive writing is like wrestling or martial arts—you need to anticipate your opponent and come up with the moves to shut him or her down. So take some time to figure out the objections readers may have to your position. You may even want to plan this out during the research stage.

Here's one method: As you're gathering evidence, fold a sheet of paper in half. Write down your latest piece of evidence in the left column. In the right column, note a possible objection a reader might raise *even after* learning about that piece of evidence. Then see if the next piece of evidence you find can answer the reader's last objection. By going left-right, left-right, you may strengthen your argument and even see the outline of your piece develop.

A memorable example is another way to get your point across. That's especially true if you want to express an idea that's abstract or one that requires a lengthy explanation. If you were trying to explain to your great-aunt what an app is, you could say it's a software program for computers and cell phones. She might not have any idea what you're talking about. If you showed her a game, a photo editor, or a music app, though, she'd probably get the gist. In writing, examples work the same way. If your piece is about cyberbullying, you'd want to include a formal definition of what it is. But to give your readers the most vivid and accurate impression, you'd also want to provide examples of what online bullies say and do.

WHAT COMES AFTER EVIDENCE?

So far, we've looked at types of evidence you can use to support your position. Maybe you're thinking, *What's all this advice about? I haven't even started writing yet!* That's true. But you'll want to be alert. That way, when you discover something that's exactly right for your piece, you'll recognize it.

CHAPTER 4

NOTES AND OUTLINE

Unless you have a photographic memory, you'll need to take notes throughout your next round of research. Many writers use computer programs that let them take notes electronically. Index cards might be old-fashioned, but they also do the trick. Experiment with different systems and use the one you're most comfortable with. As long as you can easily access the information you need and you know which source it's coming from, you're good to go. Note-taking is a tool for you as the writer—not an end in itself. No one ever published a best-selling set of notes!

WRITERS ON WRITING
Edward R. Murrow (1908-1965) was a pioneering radio and television journalist and broadcaster known for his integrity. To Murrow (left), persuasion and truthfulness went hand in hand: "To be persuasive we must be believable; to be believable we must be credible; to be credible we must be truthful. It is as simple as that."

TAKING NOTES

No matter how you take notes, here are some things to keep in mind. First, don't copy a source word for word unless you intend to include a direct quote. If you *are* using a quote, put quotation marks around it, just to be on the safe side. Sometimes when you're taking notes, it seems easiest to write the words down just as they are. You might remember to put the information in your own words later on—but after you've been taking notes for three nights straight, it's easy to lose track. Then you might end up plagiarizing the source (passing off the work of others as your own). Plagiarism isn't cool! Don't let a careless mistake ruin your credibility. Make a habit of paraphrasing as you go.

Libel is another thing to avoid. You may have heard that term on the news. What does *libel* mean, exactly? It's when someone publishes false or misleading statements that damage another person's reputation. (Statements that are spoken and not published are called "slander.") Yes, we have freedom of speech. Still, freedom of speech doesn't mean we can make things up about other people or spread rumors with no basis in fact. Libel is against the law. However, if you use reliable sources and take careful notes, it shouldn't be a problem.

TIME TO OUTLINE!

You've got a stack of note cards or a computer file full of facts. The next step is to draft an outline. Remember the map analogy? When you did your overview, you zoomed out, looking at the landmarks and highways. Now you're starting to zoom in. You're seeing street names. You might see a lake or a park that didn't appear before. You can start to plan your route—or write an outline, in other words.

An outline doesn't have to be a complicated maze of Roman numerals and As and Bs and 1s and 2s. Many writers make simple lists, with a series of main points and supporting points underneath them. You can write in full sentences or fragments—that's up to you. If you're a visual person, you could make a diagram. It's also just fine to use a method that's all your own. Your outline doesn't need to make sense to anyone else.

A STURDY STRUCTURE

As you outline, remember that there is **no one-size-fits-all structure for a persuasive piece—or for any piece of writing. Your structure depends on what you have to say.** In a formal essay, you'd use well-developed paragraphs with easily identifiable topic sentences. In a blog post, you could be less formal. Your paragraphs could be short, your thesis statement could go anywhere, and your conclusion could be bold and unexpected. When you're just starting a piece, though, focus on the basics: beginning, middle, and end.

For your audience, reading an introduction is like meeting you for the first time. Are you going to mumble and avoid eye contact? Are you going to be loud and obnoxious? Of course you won't! You are going to be confident, direct, and interesting. You're going to be the kid at the party who everyone wants to get to know.

Begin your introduction with a "hook"—an attention grabber. Signal to your reader that you've got something important to say. Many of the tools in chapter 3 work well as attention-getters. You could open your piece with a startling fact or quotation. You could begin with a thought-provoking question or anecdote. You could describe a scene as if it were the opening of a movie. You could even come up with an approach that's entirely original.

At the other end of your piece is the conclusion. The conclusion is the clincher—the place where you pull everything together. Often writers will go full circle, repeating a phrase or extending a metaphor that appeared in the introduction. Quotes are another good way to end a piece. Try to leave the reader with an image or idea that he or she just can't shake.

If you don't know yet how you want to open and close your piece, that's OK. You can skip both of those for now. When it comes to your outline, it's the middle that's most important. You need to establish a logical order for the various points that make up the middle of your piece. Luckily, you're not starting from scratch. You've been sorting your ideas all along, beginning with the brainstorming you did after gathering your research materials. By now you probably have a good idea of what your main points are, and you have evidence to support each one. Sometimes your points might be equal in importance. Most of the time, though, one or two points will stand out as being more powerful or unusual than others. Decide if these points would be best at the beginning (to start strong) or at the end (to finish strong).

As you consider your structure, remember that an outline isn't an end in itself. It's simply a handy guide—a way to keep your whole piece in mind even as you focus on one small part of it. And if your outline isn't working for you down the road, you can always change it. Make this step work for you.

WRITE IT OUT!

Are you a visual person? Use color to help you keep track of your research. Assign a color to each of your main points and then highlight the top line of your note cards. You could also doodle funny symbols. You could even make little sketches, as if you were creating a graphic novel. Visual cues can make staying organized easier—and more fun.

CHAPTER 5

HELPFUL TECHNIQUES

So far, we've covered the *why* (passion for your topic), the *what* (evidence), and the *where* (your outline) of persuasive writing. Before you go any further, let's look at the *how*. Creating a great persuasive piece isn't simply a matter of gathering and organizing information. You're not graphing a math problem—you're trying to win an argument! So let's take a look at some of the ways you can accomplish that.

SOCIAL INFLUENCE

All human beings share a need to belong. We want to feel that we're part of a group. A long time ago, people learned that to survive as a species, we have to work together and seek the common good. As a result, when the people around us are behaving in a certain way, our natural impulse is to behave the same way—unless we have a good reason not to.

  If other people are already taking the action you advocate, be sure to include that information in your piece. Describe these people in positive terms, such as *compassionate, reasonable,* or *intelligent.* Your reader will want to identify with them and be more likely to join in the effort. Fund-raising campaigns use this strategy frequently—because it works.

OVERCOME INERTIA

Another fact of human psychology is that people resist change. That tendency actually serves a purpose—think how chaotic life would be if nothing stayed the same very long! Of course, sometimes change is necessary. **If you want people to take a specific action, make sure that what you're asking them to do is as simple as possible. Then make sure that your directions are perfectly clear, with no chance of being misunderstood.**

Suppose you were writing a letter to the editor encouraging people to donate to a food drive. If at the end you wrote, "Bring your donations to the grocery store," people might ignore your letter because they wouldn't know exactly what to do. Unless you live in a very small town, they might wonder *which* grocery store. They might also wonder what kind of food the store accepts and how long the drive will last. But if you wrote, *Bring your canned and boxed food items to the Tastee Foods customer service desk between now and March 15*, more people will bring in donations.

APPEAL TO EMOTIONS

People usually think of themselves as rational beings that make decisions based on logic. But when it comes right down to it, much of what people actually *do* is based on feelings. That applies to everyone: female and male, rich and poor, educated and uneducated, young and old. As noted earlier, personal stories go a long way in making an emotional impact. However, even if you don't have a particular story to share, you can still describe your topic in a way that will persuade people to empathize with your cause. If you wish to convince people to eat less meat, for instance, you could describe the ways that farm animals are similar to cats, dogs, and other animals people keep—and love—as pets.

LEARN FROM THE MASTERS

Eric Schlosser (author of *Fast Food Nation*) and cowriter Charles Wilson combine facts, statistics, and graphic details to create emotional impact in this excerpt from *Chew on This: Everything You Don't Want to Know about Fast Food*:

Eric Schlosser (*above*) published *Chew on This* with cowriter Charles Wilson in 2006.

In 2006, about 9 billion chickens will be raised in the United States, slaughtered, and then eaten. That works out to almost thirty chickens for every man, woman, and child in the country. Killing a chicken has never been pleasant. The old-fashioned method, used by farmers for centuries, is to chop off their heads with an ax. You've probably heard that a chicken can run around for a few moments without its head. That's true, although it's not something farmers like to see. The billions of chickens slaughtered every year to make McNuggets and KFC Crispy Strips don't get a chance to run around without their heads. They are killed at enormous slaughterhouses, hanging upside down, their legs shackled to a fast-moving chain that carries thousands of birds.

Even though your piece is a work of nonfiction, a few elements of creative writing can help it reach readers' hearts. Let's say you're writing about the need for safe drinking water in underdeveloped countries. You have plenty of facts and figures, but you want your readers to be emotionally engaged. Try taking the reader through a day in the life of people affected by this crisis. Describe the long walk to the nearest safe well. Describe a family mourning a young child who died because of a waterborne disease. If you can capture a situation with the vivid language of good fiction, your readers may be more affected by it.

LOOK INTO THE FUTURE

Another creative writing technique is prognostication—in other words, looking into the future. If you believe that our dependence on technology will eventually destroy our ability to relate to one another as human beings, let readers see and hear what that might look like. Show them a nearly empty Times Square, with just a few people scattered about, using their devices instead of interacting with one another. Include a bit of dialogue in which the characters don't understand one another. Let your readers feel a little spooked! They will be more receptive to your solutions if the future you're describing alarms them.

Prognostication can also take a positive spin. You could describe all the good things that will happen if people *do* make a change. Have you studied Martin Luther King Jr.'s "I Have a Dream" speech? In 1963, speaking before an audience of about 250,000 civil rights supporters in Washington, DC, King described a world in which black children and white children would see one another as sisters and brothers—a world in which "the sons of former slaves and the sons of former slave owners will be able to sit down together at the table of brotherhood."

THE POWER OF METAPHOR

Metaphors can be another persuasive tool. This technique is also a staple of fiction. Metaphors show a similarity between two different things. (A simile—which uses *like* or *as* to compare things directly—is a particular type of metaphor.) **Metaphors can be a great way to liven up your writing—and if your prose pulls in readers, you're more likely to convince them of your viewpoint.** If, in a piece about your city's recycling program, you refer to a landfill as an "ocean of garbage that fills the horizon," your reader can visualize the vastness of the landfill.

An extended metaphor uses more than one example to make a comparison. In this case, you would continue using language related to the initial metaphor throughout your piece. In the example of the landfill, you could use words like *wave, swell, tsunami, pounding surf, undercurrents,* and so on.

Metaphors help a writer convey a lot of information in a concise, engaging way. But be careful of overdoing it. If you use too many different comparisons, they will lose their effectiveness and become a distraction.

TONE MATTERS

What you say matters a lot in a persuasive piece. So does how you say it—the tone of your piece, for instance. Tone is basically the author's attitude—toward the subject as well as the x. Word choice helps create tone. Difficult or formal words will give readers a different impression than casual words.

Let's say you are writing a letter to the editor complaining about the conditions of the restrooms at a city park. Formal words such as *foul, unclean,* or *verminous* are at one end of the scale. At the other end are words such as *sick, nasty,* or *gross.* Words such as *dirty*, *filthy*, or *grimy* fit in between. You'd want to carefully decide which words convey the tone you are trying to establish.

When writing a persuasive piece about something you have strong feelings about, it can be easy to slip into a scolding tone. You might write something like, "If you really care about animals, you should stop eating meat immediately. Don't be a hypocrite." Statements like those are blunt and clear, but the reader is likely to feel defensive—and won't want to keep reading.

Sometimes it's hard to pin down just which words or techniques create tone. Don't overthink it. Just go back to that auditorium and imagine your readers sitting in front of you. Would you be telling jokes? Impressing them with your logical analysis? Earnestly pleading your case? Once you really get into the writing, you'll probably find that an appropriate tone emerges naturally.

WRITE IT OUT!

Do you want to tune in to tone? Try this exercise. Think of a simple sentence—one that you'd say out loud to someone else. Let's say your sentence is, "Pass the potatoes." If you said that to your little brother and you were mad at him, you might say, "Give me the potatoes!" If you were speaking to your mother, you might say, "Can I have some more potatoes?" If you were at the table with your dad's boss, you might be extra polite and say, "Would you mind passing the potatoes, please? Thank you and help yourself." Try this with a few different sentences, changing the person to whom you're speaking each time.

OTHER TECHNIQUES

Why do you think questions are a good way to get your reader's attention? Is it because our automatic response is to start thinking of an answer? Even rhetorical questions—which don't require a reply—can get readers thinking. A writer making the case for hybrid school buses might begin by asking, "Would you encourage a child with asthma to sit in a room filled with secondhand cigarette smoke? Hardly! But the diesel fumes emitted by a line of idling school buses could be just as dangerous." Questions can also keep your writing from becoming monotonous. If you use this technique, though, make sure your questions are concise and focused on your topic.

LEARN FROM THE MASTERS

Malala Yousafzai (below) is an activist for education, particularly education for girls. In 2012 she defied the Taliban in Pakistan and was shot in the head. She survived and continues to speak out about the need for education. She received the Nobel Peace Prize in 2014

at the age of seventeen. In this passage from a 2012 address to the United Nations Youth Assembly, Yousafzai repeats a single word—one—to a rhythmic and inspiring effect: "So let us wage a glorious struggle against illiteracy, poverty and terrorism, let us pick up our books and our pens, they are the most powerful weapons. One child, one teacher, one book and one pen can change the world."

Repeating certain words or phrases in your piece can emphasize your point and create drama. Even if the words are simple, the repetition creates a rhythm and sets up expectations. Readers will recognize the pattern and be likely to remember what you have to say. If you were writing about the need for better educational programs for kids with attention deficit hyperactivity disorder (ADHD), you could use sentences like these:

> *Kids with ADHD need teachers who understand what it means to have this disorder. Kids need to take breaks during the day in order to do their best. They need the opportunity to try different learning strategies.*

As with metaphors, however, don't go overboard. Read your work out loud and listen closely to determine if the repetition enhances your piece or detracts from it.

Is your head spinning by now? This is a lot to keep track of! You certainly don't have to use all of these techniques. Just use the ones that make the most sense for your piece. And here's something else to keep in mind: many of these approaches will come to you as you write. Part of writing is a conscious act, but much of it is subconscious. And your subconscious already knows a lot of this stuff. Trust yourself.

CHAPTER 6

DRAFTING YOUR PIECE

Topic? Check. Research? Check. Notes? Check. Outline? Check. At long last, it's time to write!

Don't feel that you have to get things right the first time. Not even the pros can manage that. It's just a first draft—no one else has to see it. So dig in. Write longhand or go straight to the keyboard. Finish your draft in one long session or break it up into a few shorter ones. If you write best under pressure, give yourself a deadline. If you'd rather take your time, that's OK too. Keep in mind that you don't have to write your piece in any particular order. If you want to tackle your middle point first or save your intro for last, go for it.

Use your notes and outline to guide your rough draft. You can start writing at the beginning, middle, or end of your paper.

LEARN FROM THE MASTERS

The Omnivore's Dilemma: The Secrets behind What You Eat adapts Michael Pollan's well-known book about health and eating for a young audience. Author Richie Chevat begins the book by describing a familiar scene—with a mysterious twist. Doesn't this introduction make you want to keep reading?

Michael Pollan (above) published *The Omnivore's Dilemma* in 2006.

> The average supermarket doesn't seem much like a field of corn.
>
> Take a look around one. What do you see? There's a large, air-conditioned room. There are long aisles and shelves piled high with boxes and cans. There are paper goods and diapers and magazines. But that's not all. Look again. Somewhere, behind the brightly colored packaging, underneath the labels covered with information, there is a mountain of corn.
>
> You may not be able to see it, but it's there.

ON PAUSE

When you've finished your first draft, let it sit for a few days if possible. Focus on other areas of your life. Have some fun! When you look at your piece again, you'll be able to see it more clearly. Even just a short break—say, an hour or two—can give you a better perspective on your writing.

With your second or third drafts, concentrate on the structure of your piece. Now is the time to make sure there are no missing parts, that your evidence is in the right order, and that your persuasive techniques are working the way you intended. When you're confident about all of these things, you can start to fine-tune your writing.

At the top of the fine-tuning list: write lean. If you can say something using fewer words and still convey your meaning, do it. In addition, don't use difficult words when simple ones will do. The whole point of writing is to connect with the reader. It's hard to do that when the reader has a lot of extra words

WRITERS ON WRITING

Even famed novelist and essayist Toni Morrison (author of *Beloved* and *Song of Solomon*) experiences frustration while writing. But Morrison (below) also finds joy in revising her work: "Writing it all out

for the first time is painful because so much of the writing isn't very good. I didn't know in the beginning that I could go back and make it better; so I minded very much writing badly. But now I don't mind at all because there's that wonderful time in the future when I will make it better, when I can see better what I should have said and how to change it. I love that part!"

to wade through. Think of your words as having weight. Your reader is picking up each one and hanging on to it until he or she understands your meaning. If a line is too heavy—if there are too many words—the reader will get tired and may decide to bail on the whole piece.

Also pay close attention to sentence structure. A passage that uses the same structure over and over might put your reader to sleep! Vary the first words of your sentences, especially those in close succession. **As you're checking for variety, keep an eye out for passive sentences as well. In a passive sentence, an object acts upon the subject, rather than the other way around.** Writers sometimes fall back on passive sentences when they don't have all their facts or don't want to assign blame. For example, "The document was filed incorrectly" doesn't say *who* filed the document incorrectly. "The boy was chased by the security officer" is another example of passive construction. "The security officer chased the boy" would be a better choice. Both sentences have the same meaning, but the second one is more active.

IF YOU GET STUCK

It happens to just about every writer from time to time. The words aren't there, or the ideas are all tangled up in a heap and you don't know how you'll ever untangle them. Those feelings are completely normal. Even the most accomplished writers in the world struggle with self-defeating thoughts at times.

Try to pinpoint the reason you feel stuck. Maybe your mind is on other things, and you simply need to take a break. On the other hand, the problem may be about ideas. If that's the case, try outlining this draft as it is right now. Yes, you wrote one outline already, but perhaps you didn't stick to it as well as you thought—or perhaps your argument worked well in theory, but now that you've written a draft, you see errors that you can't resolve by tweaking words here and there.

These are all common situations. You didn't do anything wrong—it's part of the writing process. And you know what? Often the areas we struggle with the most end up being the best parts. We get flashes of insight that we would never have experienced if the writing had come easily in the first place.

Whatever the reason for your writer's block, here are some tips to get you back on track:

- Don't think in terms of the whole piece. Just ask yourself if there's one thing you can change— whether it's adding a single word or taking one away. Make the change. Look at your piece again. Is there one thing you can change? Soon you'll get on a roll and won't have to take small steps anymore.

- Address your piece to a particular person. It could be someone you know, or you could invent a character just for this purpose. What would you say? What questions would this person ask? Maybe writing for one particular person will open up a whole new area of your argument.

- Rekindle your passion for your topic. Why did you choose to write about lowering the voting age or your crumbling school building or the necessity of space exploration? Picture yourself leading a rally, shouting out the buzz words, and getting everyone fired up. Then get back to work!

You might be wondering how many drafts you'll need to write. That's up to you. There is no magic number! Maybe you'll nail it on the second or third draft. Maybe you'll need to write five or more drafts before your piece is ready. Every writer has his or her

WRITERS ON WRITING

For decades, writers have turned to William Zinsser (left) for advice on sharpening their skills. In this quote from *On Writing Well: The Classic Guide to Writing Nonfiction,* Zinsser describes an effective conclusion: "The perfect ending should take our readers slightly by surprise, but seem exactly right."

own process—and readers won't know if they're reading the first draft or the twentieth. What matters is that you said what you wanted to say.

Most likely, one of the last things you'll write is the first thing your readers will see: the title. Read your piece and see if a phrase or a quote really stands out. Can you think of a common saying that you could adapt to your topic? Titling your piece is another good occasion for brainstorming. Put all your ideas out there and see what happens. If you can't decide, run your best ideas by your friends or teachers and get their opinions. And you never know— sometimes the perfect title will just pop into your head.

FINAL STEPS

Once you've reached the home stretch, consider getting input from others. We all have blind spots. Find a reader and let him or her know if you have any particular questions. Keep an open

WRITE IT OUT!

A quote here. A statistic there. You know you need them in your piece, but how do you actually include them? And how do you say where your information came from without bringing your smooth prose to a screeching halt? Study the work of the pros! Take a close look at a few well-written articles from respected magazines or websites and pay attention to:

- Placement of quotation marks
- Use of phrases such as *said, according to, as stated by,* and so on
- Mention of job titles, organization names, and other official designations

Take note of all the different approaches you find and then try using them in your own piece.

mind and try not to take any negative comments personally. On the other hand, don't change something just because someone else thinks you should. Consider the advice and then make your own decision. It's your piece.

Once you've fielded a second opinion, use this checklist to make sure your piece is the best it can be. Read through the piece a few times, concentrating on different aspects each time.

- Do you have an attention-getting introduction?
- Do you state your thesis clearly?
- Do your main points support your thesis? Does your evidence support your main points?

- Are your points arranged in the best possible order?
- Does your conclusion bring your piece to a satisfying and logical end?
- Are your sources credible?
- Have you cited your sources?
- Does your piece include emotional appeal for your particular audience?
- Is the tone of your piece consistent and appropriate for the content?
- Have you repeated certain words too often?
- Do you use a variety of sentence structures?
- Have you chosen precise words and cut unnecessary words?
- Have you proofread for spelling and grammatical errors?
- If you are writing for a specific publication, have you followed the guidelines for length, format, and so on?

After checking off the items on this list, tell yourself congratulations! You have written a meaningful piece about something important to you. Be proud of it. Share it with your family, classmates, neighbors, and friends. It's time to let your persuasive powers shine.

WRITING FOR A LIVING

You've learned how to put together a knockout persuasive essay. Do you know what else you've learned? Well, we'll tell you: a whole lot of valuable skills that could someday lead to a rewarding occupation! In writing your paper, you made literally thousands of decisions, big and small. You picked a topic and sources, and then you selected your evidence. You paraphrased, summarized, and synthesized. You supported your central idea and carried it all the way through to the end. Those are important skills. More than ever, the world needs people who excel at the kinds of tasks you just did.

If you're an aspiring persuasive writer, your first thought might be to write books yourself. Maybe you'll write the next *Silent Spring*! Or maybe you'd like to write for a magazine or a website. You could be a columnist or a blogger.

But don't stop there. You can put your skills to good use in many other occupations as well. Grant writing is one example. Big organizations (government departments, corporations, and foundations) often offer funding to businesses, schools, cities, and so on. Grant writers gather and present all the information the applicants need to pursue the grant. A talented grant writer can make all the difference to a worthwhile organization.

Maybe you like combining words and images or video. Consider making documentaries. Do you like working directly with people? Consider public relations or speech writing.

Maybe your persuasive talents lean toward selling things. Consider a job in marketing, as a copywriter. Marketing isn't just about commercials on TV or slick photos in magazines. It's all around us. Just take a look at the mail in your home. Do you have any catalogs? Postcards? Requests from charitable or political organizations? These items are full of persuasive writing. Then think of all the copy you find online, such as websites and product descriptions. Someone has to write the words you see. If you want to learn more about careers in writing—well, you can research this one yourself. You know what to do!

SOURCE NOTES

8   Sue Macy, quoted in "Interview with Sue Macy, Author of *Wheels of Change*," Sporty Girl Books, August 20, 2013, http://sportygirlbooks.blogspot.com/2013/08/interview-with-sue-macy-author-of.html.

11   Kao Kalia Yang, "The Meemao Monster," *18 Million Rising*, January 11, 2015, http://18millionrising.org/blog/2015/jan/11/meemao-monster.

13   Tanya Lee Stone, quoted in "Interview with Tanya Lee Stone (Part 1)," *Ultimate YA*, March 16, 2013, http://theultimateyareadinggroup.tumblr.com/post/45525468105/interview-with-tanya-lee-stone-part-1.

15   Jackie Robinson, "Letter from Jackie Robinson to President Dwight D. Eisenhower," National Archives, May 13, 1958, http://www.archives.gov/exhibits/featured_documents/jackie_robinson_letter/images/robinson_letter_page_1.jpg.

20   Al Gore, *Our Choice: A Plan to Solve the Climate Crisis* (Emmaus, PA: Rodale, 2009), 57.

23   Alisher, quoted in Tatyana Kleyn, *Immigration: The Ultimate Teen Guide* (Lanham: Scarecrow, 2011), 133.

26   Edward R. Murrow, "The Edward R. Murrow Center of Public Diplomacy," Fletcher School—Tufts University, accessed January 16, 2015, http://fletcher.tufts.edu/murrow.

32 Eric Schlosser and Charles Wilson, *Chew on This: Everything You Don't Want to Know about Fast Food* (Boston: Houghton Mifflin, 2006), 178.

33 Martin Luther King Jr., "I Have a Dream," *American Rhetoric: Top 100 Speeches*, August 28, 1963, http://www.americanrhetoric.com/speeches/mlkihaveadream.htm.

36 Malala Yousafzai, "Malala Yousafzai: 'Our Books and Our Pens Are the Most Powerful Weapons," *Guardian* (London), July 12, 2013, http://www.theguardian.com/commentisfree/2013/jul/12/malala-yousafzai-united-nations-education-speech-text.

39 Richie Chevat and Michael Pollan. *The Omnivore's Dilemma: The Secrets behind What You Eat* (New York: Dial, 2009), 9.

40 Toni Morrison, quoted in Richard Nordquist, "Toni Morrison on Writing," *About Education,* accessed January 15, 2015, http://grammar.about.com/od/advicefromthepros/a/morrisinterview.htm.

43 William Zinsser, *On Writing Well: the Classic Guide to Writing Nonfiction*, 4th ed. (New York: HarperCollins, 1990), 76.

GLOSSARY

analysis: a close examination of the different parts that make up a whole and how these parts relate to one another

credible: able to be believed

evidence: a sign of a claim's truthfulness or falsity

metaphor: a technique in which one object is used to suggest the qualities of another object

plagiarizing: passing off someone else's writing as one's own, without giving credit

primary source: original material created at the time, place, or both that you are writing about

prognostication: the act of looking into the future

relevant: directly connected to a topic

secondary source: material created by people who weren't present for or directly involved with a topic

statistic: a numerical figure that represents a piece of information and that has been taken from a survey of data

thesis: an idea that is to be proved

SELECTED BIBLIOGRAPHY

"Analysing Persuasive Language." *Lessonbucket*, April 27, 2013. http://lessonbucket.com/english/year-9-english/persuasive-language/analysing-persuasive-language.

"Argue, Persuade and Advise." *BBC KS3 Bitesize*. Accessed January 12, 2015. http://www.bbc.co.uk/bitesize/ks3/english/writing/argue_persuade_advise/revision/3/.

Clark, Brian. "Ten Timeless Persuasive Writing Techniques." *Copyblogger,* September 26, 2007. http://www.copyblogger.com/persuasive-writing.

Harvey, Stephanie. *Nonfiction Matters: Reading, Writing, and Research in Grades 3–8*. York, ME: Stenhouse, 1998.

Larsen, Lou. "17 of the World's Most Powerful Written Persuasion Techniques." *NLP Language Patterns for Advertising* (blog), June 17, 2010. http://blog.nlp-techniques.com/2010/06/17-of-the-worlds-most-powerful-written-persuasion-techniques.

Markman, Roberta, Peter T. Markham, and Marie L. Waddell. *10 Steps in Writing the Research Paper*. Hauppauge, NY: Barron's, 2011.

Rozakis, Laurie. *Schaum's Quick Guide to Writing Great Research Papers*. New York: McGraw-Hill, 2007.

Woods, Geraldine. *Research Papers for Dummies*. New York: Hungry Minds, 2002.

Bodden, Valerie. *Write and Revise Your Project*. Minneapolis: Lerner Publications, 2015. You've been assigned to write a research project. You've done all your research. What's next? This book walks you through each step of writing and revising your work.

Loewen, Nancy. *Writing Outstanding Opinion Pieces*. Minneapolis: Lerner Publications, 2016. This appealing introduction to writing a convincing opinion piece offers useful tips to help young writers hone their skills.

Purdue Online Writing Lab (OWL)
https://owl.english.purdue.edu
Purdue University's Online Writing Lab provides writing resources for students in grades 7–12. Check out the site for tips on starting the writing process, overcoming writer's block, proofreading for errors, and much more.

Roy, Jennifer Rozines. *Sharpen Your Report Writing Skills*. Berkeley Heights, NJ: Enslow, 2012. No need to stress out! This book is a helpful guide in writing and presenting all kinds of reports. It has funny graphics too.

Terban, Marvin. *Ready! Set! Research! Your Fast and Fun Guide to Writing Research Papers That Rock!* New York: Scholastic, 2007. Using lots of examples, this book gives a fast and fun look at how to pick a subject, complete research, and write a report.

200 Prompts for Argumentative Writing
http://learning.blogs.nytimes.com/2014/02/04/200-prompts-for-argumentative-writing
If you can't decide on a topic, this list is sure to give you some ideas! Categories include education, technology and social media, arts and media, gender issues, sports, politics, parenting and childhood, health and nutrition, and morality.

Using Rhetorical Strategies for Persuasion
https://owl.english.purdue.edu/owl/resource/588/04
This site describes strategies for persuasion and includes a discussion of logical fallacies—in other words, what *not* to do when making an argument!

INDEX

PHOTO ACKNOWLEDGMENTS

The images in this book are used with the permission of:
© iStockphoto.com/samxmeg, p. 7; © Nattika/Shutterstock.com, p. 10; Courtesy Kao Kalia Yang, p. 11; © Todd Strand/Independent Picture Service, p. 13; © Mark Rucker/Transcendental Graphics/Getty Images, p. 15; © Yasonya/Shutterstock.com, p. 16; © Matthew Simmons/WireImage/Getty Images, p. 20; © Ferris, Jean Leon Gerome/Private Collection/Bridgeman Images, p. 22; © Audrey C. Tiernan Photography, Inc., p. 23; © Bettmann/CORBIS, p. 26; © Evgney Karandaev/Shutterstock.com, p. 29; © Andrew Harrer/Bloomberg/Getty Images, p. 32; © iStockphoto.com/Stitchik, p. 35; © Karwai Tang/WireImage/Getty Images, p. 36; © Kaori Ando/Image Source/Getty Images, p. 38; © Jeff Morgan 08/Alamy, p. 39; © Ian Langsdon/EPA/CORBIS, p. 40; © Walter Daran/The LIFE Picture Collection/Getty Images, p. 43; © koosen/Shutterstock.com (cardboard background); © Everything/Shutterstock.com (spiral notebook); © AtthameeNi/Shutterstock.com (grid paper); © oleschwantder/Shutterstock.com (yellow lined paper).

Cover: © koosen/Shutterstock.com (cardboard); © oleschwantder/Shutterstcock.com (yellow lined paper).

ABOUT THE AUTHOR

Nancy Loewen has published more than 120 books for children and young adults. Two of her books have been finalists for Minnesota Book Awards: *The Last Day of Kindergarten* and *Four to the Pole* (cowritten with polar explorer Ann Bancroft). Her picture book *Baby Wants Mama* was named an Oppenheim Toy Portfolio Best Book. Loewen has also received awards from The American Library Association, the New York Public Library, and the Association of Educational Publishers. She holds an MFA from Hamline University, St. Paul. Loewen was born in Mountain Lake, a small town in southern Minnesota. She lives in the Twin Cities. Visit her online at nancyloewen.com.